SPANISH 1
LIFEPAC EIG

CONTENTS

Authors: **Katherine Engle, B.A., M.A.**
                 Vicki Seeley Milunich, B.A., M.S. Ed.
Editor: Alan Christopherson, M.S.
Graphic Design: Kyle Bennett, Jennifer Davis,
                 Alpha Omega Staff

Alpha Omega Publications

Published by Alpha Omega Publications, Inc.
300 North McKemy Avenue, Chandler, Arizona 85226-2618

SPANISH 1: LIFEPAC 8
TRAVEL & TRANSPORTATION

OBJECTIVES

When you have completed this LIFEPAC, you should be able to:

1. Discuss transportation needs, including destinations and modes of transport.

2. Use the forms of **estar** to communicate location of yourself, buildings, etc.

3. Choose between the simple present and the present progressive tenses in conversation. You will recognize the use of these tenses while reading and listening to other speakers.

4. Become increasingly proficient in the use of direct object pronouns.

5. Use the reflexive verbs and pronouns in order to discuss your own personal care and hygiene.

I. VOCABULARY & GRAMMAR

Conversation

Manuela is talking with her friend Daniela about traveling.

Manuela:	¡Cuánto me gusta visitar a mi abuela!
Daniela:	A mí también. ¿Vive ella lejos de aquí?
Manuela:	Sí, está muy lejos. Estoy decidiendo como viajar a su casa.
Daniela:	Es muy divertido viajar por bicicleta.
Manuela:	No me interesa. Abuelita está viviendo unos doscientos kilometros de mi casa.
Daniela:	Por eso no puedes usar ni el metro ni puedes caminar. ¿Tienes un coche?
Manuela:	No tengo permiso de conducir. No puedo conducir una moto tampoco.
Daniela:	Y viajar por avión cuesta mucho dinero. No es practical.
Manuela:	Siempre me gustaría viajar por un barco, ¿sabes?
Daniela:	¡Creo que no es necesario esta vez!
Manuela:	Bueno, solamente me están quedando el autobús y el tren.
Daniela:	Yo prefiero el tren. Los trenes son limpios, y más rápidos.
Manuela:	Sí, Sí, Sí… Estoy comprando un billete para el sábado en la noche, para llegar a su casa el domingo por la mañana.
Daniela:	Y tu abuelita puede encontrarse contigo en la estación!
Manuela:	¡Qué plan más fantástico! Muchas gracias por la ayuda, Dani.
Daniela:	No es nada. Quizás algún día viaje contigo.

Translation

Manuela:	I like to travel to my grandmother's house so much!
Daniela:	I do too. Does she live far from here?
Manuela:	Yes, she is very far. I have to decide how to travel to her house.
Daniela:	Traveling by bike is a lot of fun.
Manuela:	I'm not interested in that. Grandma is some 200 kilometers from my house.
Daniela:	Therefore, you can't use the subway, nor walk. Do you have a car?
Manuela:	I don't have a driver's license. I can't drive a motorcycle either.
Daniela:	And to travel by airplane costs a lot of money. It's not practical.
Manuela:	I've always wanted to travel by ship, you know!
Daniela:	I don't think that's necessary this time!
Manuela:	Good, I'm only left with the bus and the train.
Daniela:	I prefer the train. Trains are clean, and faster.
Manuela:	Yes, yes, yes... I can buy a ticket for Saturday night and arrive at her house Sunday morning!
Daniela:	And your grandma can meet you at the station!
Manuela:	What a great plan! Thanks for the help, Dani.
Daniela:	It's nothing! Maybe someday I will travel with you?

Using the translation as a guide, locate and record the following Spanish expressions:

1.1

a. far from _____

b. I'm interested _____

c. to walk _____

d. a driver's license _____

e. it costs _____

f. I would like _____

g. by _____

h. trains _____

i. a ticket _____

j. the station _____

Practice this dialogue with your learning partner several times.

1.2   Make sure to pay special attention to the correct vowel sounds and where the accents are, then share the conversation with a teacher or parent.

✔ Adult check _____

Initial   Date

The Verb Forms Estar – to be

The verb **estar** (to be) is considered regular. Only the **yo** form is irregular and must be memorized along with the accents:

yo	**Estoy**	nosotros	**Estamos**
tu	**Estás**	vosotros	**Estáis**
el	**Está**	ellos	**Están**
ella	**Está**	ellas	**Están**
Ud.	**Está**	Uds.	**Están**

 If estar **translates as "to be," then the** yo **form is "I am." How do the other forms translate?**

1.3   a. Tú estás _____

b. El está _____

c. Ella está _____

d. Ud. está _____

e. Nts. estamos _____

f. Ellos están _____

g. Ellas están _____

h. Uds. están _____

SELF TEST 1

1.01 **Fill in the blank with the correct forms of** estar **(to be).** (10 pts. each)

a. Mi familia _____ en Nueva York.

b. Yo _____ en casa.

c. Marcos _____ viajando por el avión.

d. Ustedes _____ caminando al parque.

e. Tú y yo _____ contentos.

f. La clase _____ hablando demasiado.

g. Elena y su amiga _____ yendo por tren.

h. Pedro y Alonso _____ en el bote.

i. La profesora _____ frente a la clase.

j. Usted _____ comprando un billete.

Score _____

Teacher check _____
    Initial   Date

II. TRANSPORTATION VERB: *VIAJAR*

La bicicleta (la bici)

El metro

El coche, El carro, El automóvil

La motocicleta (la moto)

El avión, El aeroplano

El barco

El bote

El autobús

El tren

La estación(de)

El billete

El permiso de conducir

El pasaporte

A pie

La parada

El cheque de viajero

El camino

La calle, La avenida

La acera

Viajar

Ir

Ir en

Caminar

Montar en

Label the pictures with the Spanish word for each.

a._____

b. _____

c. _____

d. _____

e._____

f. _____

g. _____

h. _____

i. _____

j. _____

Using the verb viajar **and the corresponding pictures on page 8, make a complete sentence in Spanish stating how each person travels.**

MODEL: (el chico)   **El chico viaja por el tren.**

2.2   a. Tú   _____

           b. La madre   _____

           c. Yo   _____

           d. Usted y yo _____

           e. Ustedes   _____

           f. La familia _____

           g. Ella   _____

           h. Nosotras   _____

           i. Ellos   _____

           j. Usted   _____

Using the following vocabulary—usar **(to use),** cercano **(close),** lejano **(far)—make Spanish sentences describing what types of transport are most logically used to reach a nearby or faraway destination. Write at least eight sentences, using the** usted **form of** usar.

MODEL: (el barco)   **Usted usa el barco para ir lejano.**

2.3   a. _____

           b. _____

           c. _____

           d. _____

           e. _____

           f. _____

           g. _____

           h. _____

SELF TEST 2

2.01 Identify the pictures and write the Spanish word for each in the space provided. Don't forget to use the definite article with each (el, la). (5 pts. each)

a._____

b. _____

c._____

d. _____

e._____

f. _____

g. _____

h. _____

i.._____

j. _____

2.02   **Match the Spanish phrase to its correct English meaning.** (5 pts. each)

_____ 1. El billete   a. to ride

_____ 2. El pasaporte   b. the traveler's check

_____ 3. La estación   c. on foot

_____ 4. La parada   d. the ticket

_____ 5. El cheque de viajero   e. the road

_____ 6. El camino   f. the driver's license

_____ 7. El permiso de conducir   g. the stop

_____ 8. A pie   h. the station

_____ 9. El método de transporte   i. the means of transport

_____10. Montar   j. the passport

80 / 100

Score   _____

Teacher check _____
              Initial   Date

11

III. THE PRESENT PROGRESSIVE

Look back at the opening dialogue in Section One, particularly at the verb forms. Some of them look like this: **Estoy decidiendo.**

> **Refer to the opening dialogue on page 1 to complete the following activities.**

3.1   List more verbs similar in structure to the one above.

    a. _____

    b. _____

    c. _____

3.2   Based on your knowledge of Spanish vocabulary, deduce the infinitives from which these forms came.

    a. _____

    b. _____

    c. _____

You know, therefore, that the above forms have something to do with living, staying and buying. These verbs have been conjugated in the PRESENT PROGRESSIVE tense. It is a compound tense because it requires two words in order to conjugate each form.

3.3   What two words do you see in **estoy decidiendo**?

    a. _____

    b. _____

The first was a form of **estar**. The second form is called the PRESENT PARTICIPLE of the verb **decidir**, and it is translated as "deciding." Now, how is the PRESENT PROGRESSIVE translated? It is not necessarily different from the present tense you already know. You already know how to translate **estar**.

3.4   Within the form **estoy decidiendo**, how does **estoy** translate? _____

3.5   If **decidir** means "to decide," how do you complete the translation? _____

3.6   Since you already know that **estar** means "to be," translate the following forms into English:

    a. estoy decidiendo_____

    b. está viviendo_____

    c. están quedando _____

    d. estoy comprando _____

To form the PRESENT PROGRESSIVE tense of a verb, you must include two elements: an agreeing form of the verb **estar** and the present participle of the main infinitive.

3.7   Write the **tú** forms of the verbs you listed in exercise 3.1.

    a. _____

    b. _____

    c. _____

3.8   Write the **nts.** forms of the verbs you listed in exercise 3.1.

a. _____

b. _____

c. _____

Note how the participles stay the same no matter what the subject. **Estar** determines the subject, and the participle determines the action of the verb. It is important to remember that participles are not true verb forms (they do not pertain to any subject specifically) and cannot be used alone in a sentence. You always have to pair them up with a *form* of **estar**.

What's the difference between the two present tenses, such as **yo camino** and **yo estoy caminando**? There isn't much, really, and the two can be used interchangeably. The present progressive is generally used far less daily in conversation, and then usually to stress that an action is happening right now.

Determine the yo **forms of the following infinitives. Use the present participles given.**

3.9   a. ir (yendo)   _____

b. pasear (paseando)   _____

c. viajar (viajando)   _____

d. comer (comiendo)   _____

e. abrir (abriendo)   _____

If you know the present participle of ir **to be** yendo, **complete the conjugation of** ir **in the present progressive tense.**

3.10   yo_____   nts. _____

tú _____   vts. _____

el _____   ellos _____

ella_____   ellas _____

Ud. _____   Uds. _____

Formation of the Present Participle

As you have seen, the present participle in English ends with the suffix "-ing." In Spanish the suffixes are -**ando** and -**iendo**.

To form the present participle, drop the infinitive ending (-**ar, -er, -ir**) and add the appropriate suffix.

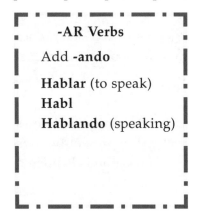

-AR Verbs

Add -**ando**

Hablar (to speak)
Habl
Hablando (speaking)

-IR/-ER Verbs

Add -**iendo**

comer (to eat)
com
comiendo (eating)

Vivir (to live)
Viv
Viviendo (living)

Irregular Participles

Some verbs have participles that do not conform to the rules, and they just have to be memorized.

IR Stem-changing ("shoe") Verbs

IR verbs that were shoe verbs in the simple present have the following changes in the stems of the present participles:

O – U	E – I
Dormir – durmiendo	vestir – vistiendo

Using the above as an example, complete this list by the given infinitives to the present participle. NOTE: These rules apply *only* to -**ir** shoe verbs. There are no changes for any other shoe verbs.

O – U

3.11   a. morir _____

E – I

b. sentir _____

c. preferir _____

d. divertir _____

e. vestir _____

f. pedir_____

Memorize the following list of irregular participles.

3.12

Ir (to go)	**yendo**
Caer (to fall)	**cayendo***
Decir (to say, tell)	**diciendo**
Oír (to hear)	**oyendo**
Poder (to be able)	**pudiendo**
Venir (to come)	**viniendo**
Leer (to read)	**leyendo**

*Any verb ending in **-aer** takes this change

✔ Adult check _____
                          Initial   Date

Complete these progressive forms by forming the present participle of each infinitive.

3.13   a. cantar   Tú estás _____

         b. beber   Nosotros estamos _____

         c. abrir   Ellos están _____

         d. escribir   Yo estoy _____

         e. gustar   Me está _____

         f. vender   Usted está _____

         g. brillar   Ustedes están _____

         h. hacer   Ella está _____

         i. salir   Las clases están _____

         j. marcharse   El se está _____

Complete this activity.

Imagine a phone call has just come through to your class, but everyone is too busy to talk. Complete the sentence, using a progressive form of the verb given, in order to state what each student is doing at the moment of the call.

3.14   a. Carlos (estudiar)   _____.

         b. Juan y Elena (escribir) _____.

         c. los chicos (leer)   _____.

         d. la chica alta (aprender) _____.

15

e. la profesora (explicar) _____.

f. yo (pensar) _____.

g. la clase (preparar) _____.

h. Tu y yo (mirar el mapa) _____.

i. Ramon (contar) _____.

j. Mariana (entender) _____.

Complete this activity.

Your family has been invited out, but everyone is too busy to accept the invitation. Explain why, using the present progressive to emphasize what they are doing now. Change the present tense forms to the corresponding progressive forms. Each of your responses should contain TWO words, the form of **estar** and the present participle. This activity may be done orally or may written out.

3.15

a. Mama lava la ropa. _____.

b. Yo estudio. _____.

c. Mi hermano limpia su cuarto. _____.

d. Elena y Papa trabajan en el garaje. _____.

e. Mi hermana no puede ir hoy. _____.

f. Pablo y yo nos vestimos hoy. _____.

g. Papa juega al golf. _____.

h. Mama lee el periodico. _____.

i. Escribo una tarea. _____.

j. Elena no prefiere visitarte. _____.

✔ Adult check _____

Initial   Date

Guided Conversation

Choose a learning partner to create this dialogue. Use the progressive verb forms as much as possible.

3.16

A. Greets you, asks if you are going to the movies on Saturday.

B. Return greeting, say you are not going to the movies. You can't.

A. Asks what you are doing instead.

B. Raul is coming to your house. You are studying for a test.

A. Asks when Raul is visiting.

B. Raul is arriving at 7:00. He is bringing another student from class, also.

A. Tell what movie you are watching.

B. Thank your partner for the invitation.

 Adult check _____
                                    Initial   Date

17

SELF TEST 3

3.01　**Give the correct forms of the verb** estar. (5 pts. each)

a. Ud. _____ aquí.

b. Nts. _____ en casa.

c. Ellos _____ en la estación.

d. Yo _____ hablando por teléfono.

e. Tú _____ contenta hoy.

3.02　**Fill in the blank with the correct progressive form of the verb given. Watch out for spelling changes and irregular verbs.** (5 pts. each)

a. cantar　　　(yo)　　　　　_____

b. vivir　　　　(Uds.)　　　　_____

c. estudiar　　(nts.)　　　　　_____

d. entender　　(tú)　　　　　_____

e. encontrar　(él)　　　　　　_____

f. tener　　　　(el hombre)　_____

g. traer　　　　(los chicos)　_____

h. estar　　　　(yo)　　　　　_____

i. saber　　　　(tú y yo)　　　_____

j. venir　　　　(Ud.)　　　　　_____

3.03　**Translate the following to Spanish.** (5 pts. each)

a. I am going by foot to the station. _____.

b. We are traveling by train. _____.

c. He is riding a bike. _____.

d. They are going by car. _____.

e. You are not traveling by boat. _____.

Score　_____

Teacher check　_____
　　　　　　　　　　Initial　　　　　　Date

18

IV. VACATIONS AND RECREATION
LAS VACACIONES Y EL RECREO

La playa

Nadar

Tomar el sol

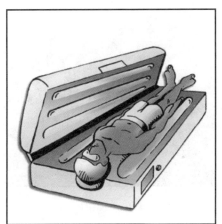

Broncearse

Pasearse en bote

Las montañas

Escalar

El alpinismo

Esquiar

El campo

Ir de camping

Montar a caballo

El mar

Pescar

La ciudad

El museo

El agente de viajeros

El/la turista

Sacar fotografías (las fotos)

For each picture below, write three Spanish sentences—two describing the action and one describing where the scene takes place. Use the vocabulary from the previous page and the given subject pronoun.

4.1   **YO:**

_____

_____

_____

4.2 **ELLOS:**

_____

_____

_____

4.3 **TÚ:**

_____

_____

_____

4.4   **NOSOTROS:**

_____

_____

_____

Conversation

> **Read the following conversation between a travel agent and a prospective tourist. Practice reading it out loud with a learning partner.**

4.5   El Agente: Buenos días, señora. ¿En qué puedo servirle?

      La turista: Buenos días. Me interesa una buena vacación para mi familia.

      El agente: Estás en el lugar correcto. Necesito un poco de información. ¿Primero, cuándo piensan viajar?

      La turista: Mi esposo y yo tenemos unas vacaciones al fin de junio.

      El agente: ¿Viajan con niños?

      La turista: Tenemos tres, un chico y dos chicas.

      El agente: ¿Cuánto tiempo vas a pasar?

      La turista: Viajamos por dos semanas.

      El agente: Yo puedo ofrecerte unas vacaciones en las montañas de Suecia. Se puede esquiar, y practicar el alpinismo.

      La turista: No, creo que no. Preferimos el calor.

      El agente: ¿Piensan quedarse en hotel?

      La turista: Sí, claro.

      El agente: ¿Cuáles intereses tiene tu familia?

      La turista: Los niños prefieren los deportes, y a mi esposo y mí nos gustan los restaurantes y los museos, los teatros, etc.

      El agente: Les interesa, quizas, una visita a la ciudad de Acapulco, Mexico. Hay muchas playas hermosas.

      La turista: Ah, y mis niños pueden tomar el sol, nadar y quizás pasearse en bote.

      El agente: Para Ustedes, hay buen turismo: los museos, varios restaurantes buenos, y todo lo interesante de una ciudad moderna.

      La turista: ¡Ay fantástico! Consigamos los billetes para el avión. No puedo esperar a decir les a mi familia.

Adult check _____

                                     Initial   Date

> **Answer the following questions about the conversation. Use complete Spanish sentences.**

4.6   a. ¿Cuándo viaja esta familia?

      b. ¿Cómo viaja?

      c. ¿Cuántos niños van?

      d. ¿Qué prefieren hacer los padres?

      e. ¿Qué desean hacer los niñios?

Create your own conversation by replacing the underlined words with ones from the vocabulary list. Rewrite the dialogue in its entirety.

4.7   Marina: A mí me gusta <u>nadar</u>.

Jorge: Y me gusta <u>tomar el sol</u>.

Marina: Debemos que <u>ir a la playa</u>.

Jorge: ¡Qué buena idea! Me encanta <u>el mar</u>.

Marina: Tú te puedes <u>broncear</u> también.

Jorge: Es divertido <u>pasearse en bote</u>.

Marina: Hay mucho que hacer a <u>la playa</u>.

_____

_____

_____

_____

_____

_____

_____

_____

_____

_____

Read the following postcards written by students to their best friends while vacationing.

4.8   Querida Consuela,

¿Qué tal? Saludos de las montañas de Colorado. Todo aquí es muy divertido. Vamos de turismo. Mi hermano y yo esquiamos casi todo el día. Mi padre escala las montañas con una guía. Yo estoy sacando muchas fotos para tí. Hace mucho frio, pero hace sol también. ¡Es una vacación perfecta!

Un abrazao fuerte,
Carlota

Querido Paco,

Escribo una tarjeta postal de las playas hermosas de California. Hace mucho sol y calor todo el tiempo. Pasamos mucho tiempo nadando en el mar. Vamos a pasearnos en bote al oceano mañana. Me encuentro con muchas chicas muy simpáticas mientras broncearme. Te veo pronto.

Tu amigo,
Enrique

✔ Adult check _____

Initial   Date

25

Verdadero o Falso (True or False).

Identify each statement as true or false, **according to the readings. Correct each false statement in the area provided below.**

4.9
a. _____ El amigo de Enrique es Carlota.

b. _____ Carlota sabe esquiar.

c. _____ Carlota viaja con su familia.

d. _____ Enrique va de camping.

e. _____ Enrique prefiere pescar.

f. _____ Hace calor en Colorado.

g. _____ Hay muchas personas en la playa.

h. _____ Carlota esquía mucho cuando va de vacaciones.

i. _____ Carlota compró un regalo para Consuela.

j. _____ No llueve mucho en California.

_____

_____

_____

_____

_____

_____

_____

_____

_____

SPANISH

ONE

LIFEPAC 8
TEST

80 / 100

Name_____

Date _____

Score _____

SPANISH I: LIFEPAC TEST 8

1. Choose elements from each column in order to complete the translations. Use the present progressive tense. (2 pts. each)

A	B	C	D
Yo	cantar	cuando	hace frío
Nosotros	divertirse	con	la cafetería
Bernardo	comer	a	temprano
Usted	vestirse	por	los amigos
Tus amigos	jugar	en	la escuela
Ella	escribir		mucho tiempo

MODEL: I am playing at school. <u>Yo estoy jugando en la escuela.</u>

a. Bernardo is having fun with his friends.

b. I am singing for a long time.

c. Your friends are eating at school.

d. You are getting dressed early.

e. She is playing when it's cold.

f. We are eating for a long time.

g. She is writing early.

h. I am getting dressed at school.

i. Your friends are eating in the cafeteria.

j. Bernardo is playing with friends.

2.   Vocabulary matching. (1 pt. each)

1. _____ The car   a. el bote
5. _____ The airplane   b. el coche
3. _____ The train   c. la motocicleta
4. _____ The subway   d a pie
5. _____ The car   e. el autobús
6. _____ The motorcycle   f. el avión
7. _____ The bicycle   g. el tren
8. _____ On foot   h. el metro
9. _____ The boat   i. la bicicleta
10. _____ The bus   j. el carro

3.   Fill in the Spanish vocabulary to complete the puzzle. (1 pt. each)

a. one day off   f. to go camping
b. to get a tan   g. to spend money
c. to ride a horse   h. mountains
d. mountain climbing   i. to ski
e. to cost   j. to take pictures

V __ __ __ __ __ __

__ __ __ __ __ __ A __ __ __

__ __ __ __ __ __ __ C __ __ __ __ __

A __ __ __ __ __ __ __ __ __ __

C __ __ __ __ __

I __ __ __ __ __ __ __ __ __

__ __ __ __ __ __ __ __ __ __ O

__ __ N __ __ __ __ __

E __ __ __ __ __ __

S __ __ __ __ __ __ __ __ __ __ __ __

2

4.	Translate the following sentences into English. Make complete sentences. (2 pts. each)

a. Voy a pie a la oficina del agente de turismo.

b. Voy en aeroplano a las montañas para esquiar.

c. Viajo en autobús al museo.

d. Me gusta ir en coche.

e. Me quedo a la playa por cuatro horas.

5.	Decide which noun was replaced by the *italicized* object pronoun in each sentence and write the correct answer in the blank. (1 pt. each)

1. *Lo* compro para mi mamá. _____
   a. los perrros	b. el regalo	c. la flor

2. En el restaurante, *las* pedimos para el almuerzo. _____
   a. la limonada	b. el jabón	c. las hamburguesas

3. ¿Vas a decir*la*? _____
   a. la verdad	b. las verdades	c. los chistes

4. Enrique *los* trae a la fiesta. _____
   a. las galletas	b. los platos	c. el postre

5. Me gusta leer*las* _____ .
   a. el periódico	b. mí	c. las revistas

6. Por favor, ¿*lo* puede dar a mí? _____
   a. el dinero	b. la computadora	c. los carteles

7. *Lo* miramos. _____
   a. Ustedes	b. mí	c. él

8. No *te* me olvidas. _____
   a. Usted	b. nosotros	c. ti

9. No *nos* ven. _____
   a. yo	b. nosotros	c. él

10. *Te* escucho bien. _____
    a. ellos	b. nosotros	c. ti

6. Choose which pronoun replaces the direct object. Place that pronoun in the correct space in each sentence—you will leave some spaces blank in each. (1 pt. each)

    a. ¿Quién sacó la bolsa?

    ¿Quién _____ sacó _____ ?

    b. Mañana tenemos un examen.

    Mañana _____ tenemos _____ .

    c. Quiero repasar la asignatura.

    Quiero _____ repasar _____ .

    d. ¿Puedes mirar a mis hermanas esta tarde?

    ¿ _____ puedes _____ mirar esta tarde?

    e. Es importante comprender las cuestiones.

    _____ es importante _____ comprender _____ .

    f. Mi padre escucha a mí.

    Mi padre _____ escucha _____ .

    g. Mi madre va a escribir a máquina el papel para mí.

    Mi madre _____ va a _____ escribir a máquina para mí.

    h. No veo a ti dentro de las multitudes.

    No _____ veo _____ dentro de las multitudes.

    i. Termino la clase a las ocho.

    _____ termino _____ a las ocho.

    j. Necesitas vender mi computadora.

    _____ necesitas _____ vender.

7.   Fill in the blank with the correct direct object pronoun for the English sentence. (1 pt. each)

       a. We use it (m.s).   _____ usamos.

       b. You ask for them (f.p.)   _____ pides.

       c. I sold it (f.s.)   _____ vendí.

       d. He visits her.   _____ visita.

       e. I need all of you.   _____ necesito.

8.   Answer the following questions in complete Spanish sentences, replacing the direct object with a pronoun. Be careful to use the correct verb form in your answer. (1 pt. each)

       a. ¿Vas a traer los cuadernos a la clase?

       b. ¿En un sánwich, prefieres la mayonesa?

       c. ¿Es necesario escribir los exámenes con el bolí?

       d. ¿Cuándo leen Uds. el periódico?

       e. ¿No vas a visitar a mí hoy?

9.   Read the following passage. Answer the following questions regarding the passage in complete, Spanish sentences. (1 pt. each)

Cuando voy de vacaciones, me gusta gastar mucho dinero. Ahorro el dinero por todo el año. Hoy, decido a donde me gustaría viajar. Es difícil. Las montañas ofrecen el esquiar y el alpinismo. El campo de las montañas es hermoso. Puedo tolerar el tiempo frío tambien. Y si voy a Suecia, voy a necesitar un pasaporte. Pero ir de camping es divertido tambien. Me divierto en el campo, y puedo practicar mi pasatiempo favorito: sacar fotografías. Ir de camping cuesta menos tambien, y puedo traer a unos amigos conmigo. Mis amigos y yo podemos ir en bicicleta por el bosque, y pescar. Puedo ir en coche al campo si voy. Pero ¿a quién no le gusta el calor de la playa? El mar siempre es bonito. Uno puede nadar, broncearse, ir en bote y descansar. Las playas de Mexico son fantásticas. Puedo viajar a Acapulco y ir de compras tambien (y gastar mucho dinero). Tengo que ir en avión a Mexico. No me gusta mucho, y cuesta mucho.

Parece que voy de camping. Puedo ir cualquier día en el verano. Es divertido quedarme con mis amigos durante las vacaciones tambien. Puedo gastar mi dinero por otro viaje el año próximo.

a. ¿Por qué le gusta viajar esta joven?

b. ¿A dónde piensa viajar (hay tres puntos de interés)?

c. ¿Por qué le gustan las montañas?

d. ¿Es de Suecia esta joven? ¿Por qué?

e. ¿Le gusta ir de camping? ¿Con quién va?

f. ¿Dónde puede gastar muchísimo dinero?

g. ¿Qué ofrece Mexico?

h. ¿Por qué no viaja a Mexico?

i. ¿Por fin, a dónde decide viajar para las vacaciones?

j. ¿En cuál estación va de camping?

10. Using the picture above, write a composition of TEN complete Spanish sentences. Describe who is in the picture and what they are doing. You may also choose to describe the weather, the setting, etc. (1 pt. each)

a. _____

b. _____

c. _____

d. _____

e. _____

f. _____

g. _____

h. _____

i. _____

j. _____

SELF TEST 4

4.01   **Match the Spanish phrase to its correct English meaning.** (2 pts. each)

_____ 1. las montañas   a. (the) recreation

_____ 2. el recreo   b. (the) city

_____ 3. esquiar   c. to fish

_____ 4. la ciudad   d. to spend

_____ 5. el alpinismo   e. (the) mountains

_____ 6. gastar   f. to tan oneself

_____ 7. broncearse   g. to ski

_____ 8. pescar   h. the sea

_____ 9. el mar   i. (the) mountain climbing

_____ 10. el/la turista   j. the tourist

4.02   **Translate the following to English.** (2 pts. each)

a. montar a caballo _____

b. pasearse en bote _____

c. quedarse _____

d. el campo _____

e. por _____

4.03   **Translate the following to Spanish.** (2 pts. each)

a. to cost _____

b. to swim _____

c. to take photographs _____

d. the travel agent _____

e. to go camping _____

4.04   **Next to each vacation site, write two appropriate activities in Spanish.** (2 pts. each)

a. la playa _____

b. las montañas _____

c. la ciudad _____

d. el mar _____

e. el campo _____

4.05 **Translate the first five sentences Spanish to English. Translate the second five sentences from English to Spanish. Use complete sentences and verb forms.** (5 pts. each)

a. La turista gasta mucho dinero.

b. Me quedo en las montañas por dos semanas.

c. El agente de viajeros va de vacaciones a la playa.

d. No saca fotografías al museo.

e. Hay muchos puntos de interés en la ciudad.

f. I go camping when I go on vacation.

g. The tourist doesn't fish.

h. We stayed in the city for five days.

i. I don't sunbathe at the beach.

j. Do vacations cost much?

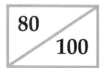

Score _____

Teacher check _____
Initial   Date

V. GRAMMAR: DIRECT OBJECT PRONOUNS

Compare the following pairs of sentences.

Example 1: **Yo tengo la tarea esta noche.** I have homework tonight.
            Yo la tengo esta noche.   I have it tonight.

Example 2: **Ella quiere un regalo.**   She wants a gift.
            Ella lo quiere.   She wants it.

In each pair, some words were replaced.

Refer to the sentences above to answer the following questions.

5.1 a. In the first example, which word was replaced?_____

     b. In the second example, which word was replaced?_____

     c. By which words were they replaced?_____

     d. What kind of words (in English) replace proper nouns? _____

     e. What parts of speech are **la** and **lo**? _____

5.2 a. What was the number and gender of the noun replaced by **la**? _____

     b. What was the number and gender of the noun replaced by **lo**? _____

5.3 Think of some other nouns that match **la** in number and gender.

     a. _____

     b. _____

     c. _____

5.4 Think of some other nouns that match **lo** in number and gender.

     a. _____

     b. _____

     c. _____

5.5 What if the nouns in the phrases above were plural?

     a. Write the pronoun that would replace **las tareas**. _____

     b. Which pronoun would replace **los regalos**? _____

5.6 Think of some other nouns that match **las** in number and gender.

     a. _____

     b. _____

     c. _____

5.7 Think of some other nouns that match **los** in number and gender.

     a. _____

     b. _____

     c. _____

29

You have just practiced the first rule of object pronouns.

Rule 1: **The direct object pronoun must agree in number, gender and meaning with the noun it replaces.**

Let's continue. Refer back to the original sentences:

Yo tengo la tarea esta noche.   **Ella quiere el regalo.**
Yo la tengo.   **Ella lo quiere.**

5.8   a. Identify the verb in each sentence. _____

        b. Identify the subjects. _____

Now look at the sentences. You can see that the placement of object pronouns within a sentence is directly IN FRONT of a VERB FORM. This is the opposite of the English, and you must work to memorize the placement.

 Replace the necessary nouns with an agreeing pronoun. Follow the original models above.

5.9   a. Ellos prefieren las hamburguesas.   Ellos _____ prefieren.

           They prefer hamburgers.   They prefer them.

        b. Necesito los libros azules.   _____ necesito.

           I need the blue books.   I need them.

        c. Uds. Compran un perro.   Uds. _____ compran.

           You buy a dog.   You buy it.

        d. Tú miras la televisión.   Tú _____ miras.

           You watch TV.   You watch it.

        e. Ella escribe una carta.   Ella _____ escribe.

           She writes a letter.   She writes it.

In each of these sentences mark an "X" where you would place an object pronoun.

5.10   a. Yo   veo   las   flores.

        b. Mañana,   vamos   a   buscar   el   correo.

        c. No   quieres   un   postre.

        d. Manolo   y   tu   prefieren   bailar.

        e. Necesito   leer   el   periódico.

        f. Por   toda   su   vida   escribe   las   novelas.

        g. Ellos   venden   los   coches.

30

Rule 2: Object pronouns can always be placed IN FRONT of a verb FORM.

How do you identify which word will be omitted and then replaced with a pronoun?
The direct object of a verb will always answer the question "**what**" or "**who**" receives the action of the verb. Let's look at our base sentences again:

Yo tengo la tarea.   **Ella quiere un regalo.**

Ask yourself: What do I have?   **Ask yourself: What does she want?**

The answers are obvious: **homework** and a **gift**. Therefore, "**la tarea**" and "**un regalo**" are the direct objects.

Using the sentences from the previous exercise, identify the direct objects by asking "who" or "what" for each. Circle them.

5.11   a. Yo veo las flores.

           b. Mañana, vamos a buscar el correo.

           c. No quieres un postre.

           d. Manolo y tú prefieren bailar.

           e. Necesito leer el periódico.

           f. Por toda su vida escribe novelas.

           g. Ellos venden los coches.

Now rewrite the sentences, eliminating the proper noun and placing the object pronoun in the correct spot.

5.12   a. _____

           b. _____

           c. _____

           d. _____

           e. _____

           f. _____

           g. _____

Now we are left only with three more pronouns: the ones that mean "me," "you" and "us." Here are all the direct object pronouns:

ME (a mí)	**NOS** (a nosotros)
TE (a ti)	
LO **LA** (a Ud. – Singular Nouns)	**LOS** **LAS** (a Uds. – Plural Nouns)

*Please take note that **lo/los** and **la/las** also translate as "you" (formal) because they replace the proper nouns **Usted** and **Ustedes**.

Look at these three sentences:

Voy a mirar la televisión.	I'm going to watch TV.
La voy a mirar.	I'm going to watch it.
Voy a mirarla.	I'm going to watch it.

There is no difference in meaning between the last two sentences. They are just two ways to express the same thing. Decide which expression you prefer and then stick with it for all your writing and speaking. That way you will avoid confusion.

Rule 3: Object pronouns may also be placed at the end of an infinitive (a verb ending in -AR, -ER, -IR).

Let's summarize the rules:

1. Direct object pronouns must agree in meaning, number and gender with the nouns they replace.
2. Direct object pronouns may be placed directly IN FRONT of a verb FORM.
3. Object pronouns may also be placed at the end of an infinitive (a verb ending in -AR, -ER, -IR).

 The direct object pronoun has been underlined in each sentence. Circle the correct proper noun it must have replaced.

5.13

1. Usualmente, mi mamá <u>los</u> lava.

   a. las hijas   b. a mí   c. los platos

2. El niño enojado <u>lo</u> golpea.

   a. a nosotros   b. a su hermano   c. la mesa

3. A ella le gusta visitar<u>las</u>.

   a. a.Ustedes   b. a la prima   c. a ti

4. No <u>nos</u> desean ayudar.
    a. a nosotros   b. a ellos   c. a ellas

5. <u>Te</u> veo mañana.
    a. el perro.   b. a Usted.   c. a ti

6. Yo <u>los</u> llevo a la escuela.
    a. la tarea.   b. los zapatos.   c. los libros

7. El jueves, <u>la</u> hago.
    a. la tarea   b. las tareas   c. a mí

8. ¿No <u>las</u> puede oír?
    a. la clase   b. los estudiantes   c. las amigas

9. Es imposible escribir<u>lo</u>
    a. el libro   b. la carta   c. las novelas

10. Me <u>lo</u> olvidé.
    a. los mensajes   b. a Ustedes   c. el mensaje

Fill in the blanks by replacing the object with the correct pronoun and writing that pronoun in the blank.

5.14   a. Yo visito a ti por la mañana.   Yo _____ visito por la mañna.

    b. Ellos necesitan la tarea de Ud.   Ellos _____ necesitan.

    c. No puede oír a mí.   No puede oír _____ .
        No _____ puede oír.

    d. Ellos no bailan la macarena.   Ellos no _____ bailan.

    e. Damos las revistas a Ustedes.   _____ damos a Ustedes.

    f. Tú ves a nosotros los lunes.   Tú _____ ves los lunes.

    g. Necesito a Ud. para ayudar.   _____ necesito para ayudar.

    h. No quiero lavar los coches de mis padres.   No _____ quiero lavar.
        No quiero lavar _____ .

    i. Me gusta escuchar la radio.   Me _____ gusta escuchar.
        Me gusta escuchar _____

    j. El miércoles, compran las camisetas.   El miércoles, _____ compran.

Identify the direct object in each sentence by circling it. Then underline the verb form. Finally, rewrite the sentence entirely, replacing the direct object with its appropriate pronoun.

5.15   a. Mi abuela visita a mi mamá todas Las Navidades.

        b. ¿Por favor, puedes repetir la cuestión otra vez?

        c. No necesitan la ayuda ahora, gracias.

        d. Me gusta ver a ti con frecuencia.

        e. Escribimos mucha tarea en la clase de español.

        f. Estudio los libros de Huidobro.

        g. Montas a motocicleta.

        h. El chófer coge a ti y a mí a las siete.

        i. No quiero una ensalada con la cena.

        j. El hermano va a lavar al perro.

        k. Mi familia invitan a Ustedes.

Reading Comprehension

Read the following passage carefully:

Es necesario preparase bien para divertirse de las vacaciones, especialmente cuando viaja una larga distancia. Debe tener los documentos importantes: el pasaporte y el permiso internacional de conducir (si intenta alquilar un automóvil). Los va a llevar constantemente por el extranjero.

Hace una lista de la ropa , las medicinas, los cosméticos y cualquier equipaje que piensa usar. La debe escribir una semana antes de partir. Es muy importante tener las recetas. Es posible que no las pueda obtener en el extranjero. Considera el tiempo, tambien. Aunque haga buen tiempo por lo general, es útil traer un ropaje diferente en caso de una tempestad, el frío, etc. Cuidado de no traer demasiadas maletas. Es difícil llevarlas, y es más posible que las pierda.

Es buena idea estudiar el país a cual visita antes de viajar. Conocerlo mejor garantiza que no se aburre porque ya sabrás qué hay para entretenerse. Será lástima que aprendiera que no hay buenas playas cercanas si le gusta nadar.

Por fin, planea arrivar al aeropuerto (la estación) una hora temprano. Dése bastante tiempo para corregir cualquieras problems que haya, facturar el equipaje y encontrar su puerta. No se necesita mucho estrés al momento de departir. Embarcar sin problemas garantiza una vacación de descanso y diversión.

Using the passage above, answer the following questions in complete Spanish sentences.

5.16   a. ¿Cuáles documentos necesita Usted para viajar al extranjero?

       b. ¿Qué puede hacer para recordar las necesidades?

       c. ¿Cuándo es bueno para escribir la lista?

       d. ¿Por qué es mala idea traer muchas maletas?

       e. ¿Cómo puede evitar aburrirse?

       f. ¿Cuándo debes llegar al aeropuerto?

       g. ¿Qué necesitas hacer en el aeropuerto antes de salir?.

       h. ¿A quién se dirige este párrafo?

Composition

Complete these writing activities.

5.17   a. Write a composition of five complete Spanish sentences describing what a tourist agent does.

_____

_____

_____

_____

_____

_____

_____

_____

b. Write a composition of ten complete Spanish sentences describing your dream vacation. You may include a description of the location in addition to outlining what activities you would do.

_____

_____

_____

_____

_____

_____

_____

_____

_____

_____

_____

_____

_____

_____

_____

_____

Adult check _____
                        Initial   Date

Conversation

You wish to go abroad for the summer as an exchange student. You need to convice your parents that this is worthwhile. Act out the dialogue with a learning partner.

5.18

A. Tell your mother you want to study in Mexico.

B. Asks when you would go and for how long.

A. Tell her you are going during the summer for six weeks.

B. Asks why you are interested.

A. Respond that you want to learn Spanish, as well as the native culture.

B. Asks what you would need.

A. Respond that you need a passport and plane tickets. You will live with a Mexican family in their home.

B. Responds that it seems (**parece**) fantastic, but it must cost a lot of money.

A. Respond that the trip costs one thousand dollars.

B. Responds that there will be other expenses (**gastos**). You are going to need new clothes, money for spending, and money for the telephone.

A. Offer to work after school and save the extra money.

B. Says she will discuss it with your father. She thinks it's a good idea.

A. Promise to work hard.

✓ Adult check _____

SELF TEST 5

5.01   **Rewrite the Spanish sentences to complete the translations.** (6 pts. each)

a. Ellas miran la televisión desmasiado: They watch IT too much.

b. Visito a mi familia los domingos: I visit THEM on Sundays.

c. No nos gustan los juegos electrónicos: We don't like THEM.

d. ¡Oímos a Uds!: We hear YOU

e. El besó a ella: He kissed HER.

f. Ven a nosotros: They see US.

g. ¿Hiciste la tarea?: You did IT?

h. Conduzco a ti al museo: I drive YOU to the museum.

i. Vas a buscar a mí en la ciudad: You are going to look for ME in the city.

j. Di a Usted el cheque: I gave IT to you.

5.02   **Answer the following questions in Spanish. Be careful to use the appropriate direct object pronoun in each answer. Note:** Some answers may take a pronoun different from the question. (8 pts. each)

a. ¿Necesitas un bolí para hacer la tarea?

b. ¿Cuándo van a visitar a mí Ustedes?

c. ¿Siempre tomas el autobús a la escuela?

d. ¿Dónde puedo encontrar a Usted?

e. ¿Hacen Uds. la torta para la fiesta?

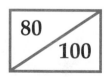

Score _____

Teacher check _____
                    Initial   Date

VI. GEOGRAPHY OF SPAIN

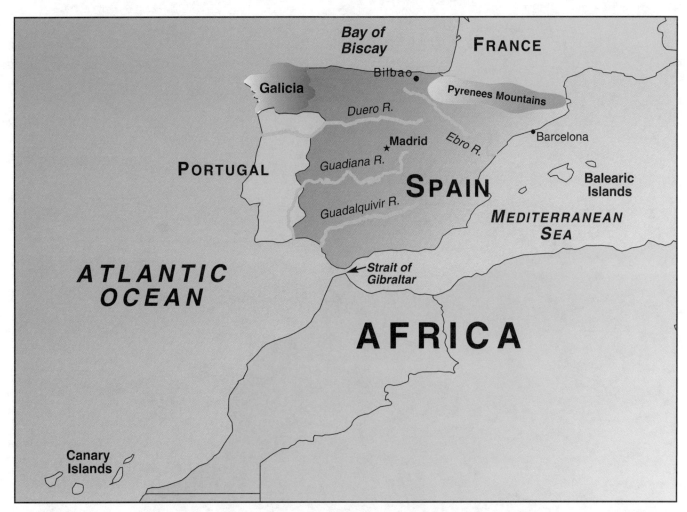

MADRID: Capital and largest city in Spain. Regarded for many years as the political, economical and cultural center of the country. Castillian Spanish is spoken here.

BILBAO: Center of Basque region. The Basque language is spoken here. Citizens of the Basque region do not consider themselves "Spanish" as such, and have long fought for independence from Spain.

BARCELONA: Site of the 1990 Olympic Summer Games. An important port city. Also known for as an artistic center of the country, as artists such as Miro and Gaudi lived and worked there. The Catalan language is spoken here.

GALICIA: Gallego spoken here.

GUADALQUIVIR RIVER: The only navigable river in Spain.

THE RIVERS DUERO, EBRO, GUADIANA: Largely unnavigable, although useful for generating electric power.

THE PYRENEES MOUNTAINS: Form the border between France and Spain.

THE STRAIT OF GIBRALTAR: The narrow passage of water between Spain and the African continent.

PORTUGAL: The country west of Spain. Separated by mountainous, rough terrain. Portuguese is spoken there.

IBERIAN PENINSULA: Land mass that includes Spain and Portugal, surrounded by water: to the east, the Mediterranean Sea; to the west, the Atlantic Ocean; to the north, the Bay of Biscay; to the south, the strait of Gibraltar.

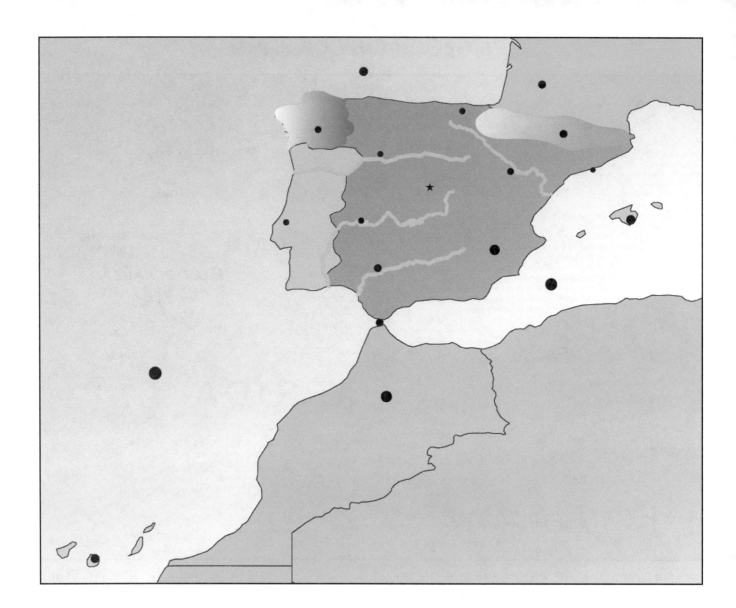

 Locate and label the following points on the map above.

6.1
a. Spain	b. France	c. Portugal
d. Mediterranean Sea	e. Bay of Biscay	f. Atlantic Ocean
g. Africa	h. Pyrenees Mountains	i. Guadalquivir River
j. Guadiana River	k. Ebro River	l. Duero River
m. Madrid	n. Barcelona	o. Bilbao
p. Balaeric Islands	q. Canary Islands	r. Strait of Gibraltar
s. Galicia		

Without looking at your map, label each of these places as river, city, country **or** land mass.

6.2 a. Barcelona: _____

b. Duero: _____

c. Pyrenees: _____

d. Barcelona: _____

e. Galicia: _____

f. Guadalquivir: _____

g. Portugal: _____

h. Canary: _____

i. Bilbao: _____

j. Ebro: _____

Answer the following questions.

6.3 a. What is the name of the entire peninsula on which Spain is located?

b. What is the capital of Spain?

c. How many different languages are spoken on the Iberian Peninsula?

d. Which river in Spain is the only navigable one?

e. What continent is south of Spain?

f. What body of water is to the north of Spain?

g. What country is west of Spain?

h. What country is north of Spain?

i. What mountain chain forms the northern border of Spain?

j. Which city is an important port?

Verdadero o falso. Decide if the statements are true or false and write V or F in the blank. In the space provided below correct the false statements. Do as many as you can without looking at the map, then use the map to complete the ones you weren't sure of.

6.4

a. _____ The Duero River is the only navigable river in Spain.

b. _____ Galicia is the capital of Spain

c. _____ The Mediterranean Sea is east of Spain.

d. _____ France is west of Spain.

e. _____ Africa and Spain are separated by the Strait of Gibraltar.

f. _____ The Iberian Peninsula contains Spain and Portugal.

g. _____ Catalan is spoken in Bilbao.

h. _____ The Pacific Ocean is west of Spain.

i. _____ Gallego is also spoken in Galicia.

j. _____ Madrid is the capital of Spain.

Note: This section does not have a Self Test.

VII. REVIEW EXERCISES

Choose the correct form of estar **in order to complete the sentences.**

7.1
1. Los niños _____ bailando.
   a. estoy   b. estamos   c. están

2. Yo _____ contento en casa.
   a. estoy   b. estás   c. está

3. María y yo no queremos _____ en el hospital.
   a. estamos   b. estoy   c. estar

4. La familia Marueca _____ aquí.
   a. está   b. estás   c. están

5. Usted va a _____ desilusionada al oír las noticias.
   a. estar   b. están   c. está

6. Usted y Usted _____ sorprendidos.
   a. está   b. están   c. estamos

7. ¿Cuándo _____ tú a la universidad?
   a. estás   b. estoy   c. estamos

8. ¿No _____ los estudiantes en la biblioteca hoy?
   a. están   b. estás   c. estoy

9. Nosotros _____ furiosos contigo.
   a. están   b. estamos   c. estar

10. Ud. _____ en España por dos semanas.
    a. estar   b. estoy   c. está

Complete the translations. Follow the model.

MODEL:	comer (to eat)	Yo estoy comiendo.	I am eating.
7.2	a. vivir (to live)	Ellos están viviendo.	_____
	b. cantar (to sing)	Tú estás cantando.	_____
	c. ser (to be)	Ellos están siendo.	_____
	d. morirse (to die)	Se está muriendo.	_____
	e. leer (to read)	Ud. está leyendo.	_____
	f. conducir (to drive)	Ella está conduciendo.	_____
	g. caerse (to fall)	Paco está cayéndose.	_____
	h. servir (to serve)	Nts. Estamos sirviendo.	_____
	i. encontrar to find)	Uds. Están encontrando.	_____

Fill in the blank with the participle.

7.3   a. (hablar)   Yo estoy _____.

 b. (entender)   El no está _____.

 c. (dar)   Uds. No están _____.

 d. (traer)   Tú estás _____ el postre.

 e. (dormir)   Todavía él está _____.

 f. (escupir)   Ellos están _____ por la ventana.

 g. (vestirse)   Mi hermana se está _____ en el dormitorio.

 h. (tener)   ¿Estamos _____ un examen?

 i. (escribir)   Mi abuela está _____ me una carta.

 j. (divertirse) Ellos van porque no se están _____.

Given the infinitive, write the correct progressive form for that verb. (Your answer should have _two_ words.)

7.4   a. vender   (ellos)   _____

 b. vestir   (Carmen)   _____

 c. tener   (yo)   _____

 d. pagar   (Ud.)   _____

 e. conocer   (Ud. y Ud.)   _____

 f. ir   (tú)   _____

 g. llegar   (nts.)   _____

 h. distribuir   (ella)   _____

 i. estar   (tú y yo)   _____

Fill in the blanks with the direct object pronouns.

7.5   (yo)   a. _____   (nts.)   d. _____

 (tú)   b. _____   (ellos, ella, Ustedes)   e. _____

 (él, ella, Usted)   c. _____

Replace the underlined object with the correct pronoun.

7.6   a. Marcos come **las galletas**.   Marcos _____ come.

b. Yo busco **mis llaves**.   Yo _____ busco.

c. Uds. No prefieren **el cine**.   Uds. No _____ prefieren.

d. El lunes, mamá espera **el autobús**.   El lunes, mamá _____ espera.

e. ¿Por qué miras a **mí**?   ¿Por qué _____ miras?

f. Veo a **ti** el domingo.   _____ veo el domingo.

g. Compran **el ropaje**.   _____ compran.

h. ¡Qué bueno! Encontraste a **nosotros**.   ¡Qué bueno! _____ encontraste.

i. Limpio **el suelo** para mi mamá.   _____ limpio para mi mamá.

j. Cuelgan **las banderas** para la fiesta.   _____ cuelgan para la fiesta.

Find and replace the direct object in each sentence with the appropriate direct object pronoun. Rewrite the sentence below.

7.7   a. Yo quiero dar el dinero a la iglesia.

b. Elena escribe a máquina la tarea.

c. ¿Oyes tú el teléfono?

d. La madre cocina las cenas.

e. ¿Dónde va Ud. a poner los dulces y las galletas?

f. El turista hace su maleta.

g. Mis tíos visitan a mí el sábado.

h. ¿Pueden Uds. ayudar a nosotros?

i. Ella no puede ver a Uds.

j. Lo siento, no puedo oír a ti.

Choose ten of the fifteen locations below. Locate and label them on the map.

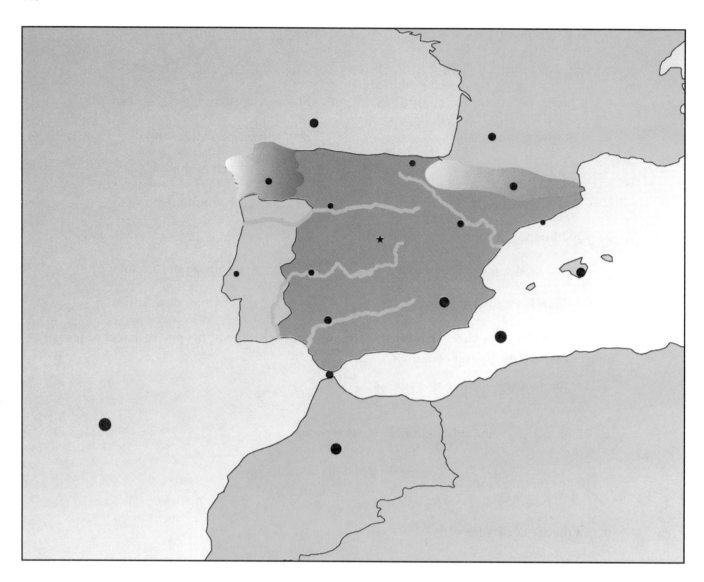

Pyrenees Mountains	Bilbao	Madrid
Strait of Gibraltar	Barcelona	Guadalquivir River
Mediterranean Sea	Portugal	France
Spain	Bay of Biscay	Duero River
Africa	Atlantic Ocean	Galicia

Note: This section does not have a Self Test.

VIII. VOCABULARY DRILL

Weather

Write three sentences in Spanish describing the weather in each scene. One of your sentences should approximate the temperature.

8.1

a._____

_____

_____

_____

_____

_____

_____

b._____

_____

_____

_____

_____

_____

_____

c._____

_____

_____

_____

_____

_____

_____

Personal Care Vocabulary

 Complete the sentences, in Spanish, with a personal hygiene item such as soap, shampoo, etc.

8.2   a. Me baño con _____.

b. Me miro en _____.

c. Me cepillo con _____.

d. Me peino con el _____.

e. Me maquillo con _____.

f. Me seco con _____.

g. Me cepillo los dientes con _____.

h. Me afeito con _____.

i. Me seco el pelo con _____.

j. Me lavo el pelo con _____.

 Write the letter of the correct translation of each verb.

8.3   1. vestirse _____

    a. to get dressed   b. to bathe   c. to go to bed

2. acostarse _____

    a. to wake up   b. to get up   c. to go to bed

3. divertirse _____

    a. to have fun   b. to shave   c. to dry off

4. levantarse _____

    a. to wake up   b. to get up   c. to wash

5. ponerse a dieta _____

    a. to go on a diet   b. to put on   c. to go

6. quitarse _____

    a. to take off   b. to get dressed   c. to look at

7. irse _____

    a. to eat lunch   b. to leave   c. to shower

8. cenarse _____

    a. to eat supper   b. to eat breakfast   c. to eat lunch

48

9. **bajarse de peso** _____

    a. to gain weight   b. to lose weight   c. to go on a diet

10. **secarse** _____

    a. to dry off   b. to take off   c. to put on

Demonstrative Adjectives

Change the given adjectives to agree with the noun in the sentence. Write your answer in the blank.

8.4
  a. (aquel)   Me gusta _____ casa.

  b. (este)   Es _____ computadora para ti.

  c. (ese)   Prefiero _____ suéteres.

  d. (este)   Mami, por favor compras _____ juguetes.

  e. (aquel)   El escala _____ árboles.

  f. (ese)   _____ chica es mi hermana.

  g. (ese)   Y _____ chico es mi hermano.

  h. (este)   ¿Por qué necesitas _____ lápiz?

  i. (aquel)   _____ montañas son muy hermosas.

  j. (este)   Estoy dando los regalos a _____ mujeres.

Fill in the blanks with the correct, agreeing demonstrative adjective.

8.5
  a. Quiero comer _____ tacos. (these)

  b. ¿Puedes ayudarme con _____ tarea? (this)

  c. No ves _____ automóviles allá? (those, far away)

  d. ¿Quién dio _____ bolígrafos a Ud? (those, close by)

  e. La tienda no vende _____ revistas. (those, close by)

  f. Visito _____ lago durante los veranos. (that, far away)

  g. No voy a comprar _____ manzana. (this)

  h. Practicamos la tarea en _____ computadora. (that, close by)

  i. _____ coche no funciona bien. (this)

  j. Asistes a _____ escuela. (that, far away)

Reflexive Verbs

 Complete the translations. Follow the model.

MODEL: Yo me lavo.   I wash MYSELF.

8.6   a. Ellos se visten.   They dress _____.

           b. Tú te pones el suéter.   You put a sweater on _____.

           c. Usted se baña.   You bathe _____.

           d. Nosotros nos miramos.   We look at _____.

           e. Ella se seca.   She dries _____ off.

           f. Ellas se pintan.   They put makeup on _____.

           g. Ustedes se quitan.   All of you take off _____.

           h. Nosotros nos divertimos.   We enjoy _____.

           i. Yo no me pongo a dieta.   I don't put _____ on a diet.

           j. Tú te levantas.   You get _____ up.

Fill in the blanks with the agreeing reflexive pronoun.

8.7   a. Enrique _____ pone el sombrero.

           b. Mi mamá _____ ducha por la noche.

           c. ¿Vas a quitar_____ los zapatos?

           d. Yo prefiero secar_____ el pelo antes de irme.

           e. Nosotros _____ divertimos mucho a la fiesta.

           f. ¿Ud. no quiere aumentar_____ de peso?

           g. Mi hermano _____ mira en el espejo mucho.

           h. Tú tienes que lavar_____ las manos con el jabón.

           i. Ustedes _____ van rápidamente del teatro.

           j. Nosotros _____ desayunamos a las siete de la mañana.

Fill in the blanks with the correct form of the given reflexive verb. (Make sure your answer has *two* words!)

8.8   a. afeitarse (él)   _____

           b. acostarse (yo)   _____

c. lavarse (Nts.) _____

d. vestirse (tú) _____

e. mirarse (Ustedes) _____

f. irse (ellos) _____

g. cenarse (Manuela) _____

h. despertarse (Usted) _____

i. bajarse de peso (las señoras) _____

j. almorzarse (tú y yo) _____

Change the reflexive verb form to agree with the new subject. (Make sure to change the pronoun and the verb form.)

8.9

a. me baño   Nosotros _____

b. se viste   Yo _____

c. nos almorzamos   Tú _____

d. se divierten   Ud. _____

e. te afeitas   Ella _____ las piernas

f. me acuesto   Uds. _____

g. se lavan   Nosotros _____

h. nos vamos   Yo _____

i. se aumenta   Ellos _____

j. me ceno   Tú _____

Change the adjectives below to the feminine. Write that form on the first blank. Then add the adverbial ending -mente to form the adverb. Write the adverb on the second blank.

8.10

a. alto _____ _____

b. sospechoso _____ _____

c. gracioso _____ _____

d. elegante _____ _____

e. caliente _____ _____

f. poderoso _____ _____

g. enojado _____ _____

h. débil _____ _____

i. dichoso _____ _____

j. tortuoso _____ _____

Note: This section does not have a Self Test.

LIFEPAC 8: VOCABULARY LIST

Nouns:

El aeroplano	the airplane
El agente de viajeros	the travel agent
El alpinismo	the mountain climbing
La acera	the sidewalk
El automóvil	the car
La bicicleta (la bici)	the bike
El billete	the ticket
El bote	the boat
La calle	the street
El camino	the road
El campo	the country
El carro	the car
El cheque de viajero	the traveler's check
La ciudad	the city
El coche	the car
La estación	the station
El mar	the sea
El metro	the subway
La motocicleta (la moto)	the motorcycle
Las montañas	the mountains
El museo	the museum
La parada	the stop
El pasaporte	the passport
El permiso de conducir	the driver's license
La playa	the beach
Los puntos de interés	the points of interest
El tren	the train
El/la turista	the tourist

Verbs:

broncearse	to tan
costar	to cost
escalar	to climb
esquiar	to ski
gastar dinero	to spend money
ir de camping	to go camping
ir	to go
ir en	to go by
ir en bote	to go by boat
montar a caballo	to ride a horse
nadar	to swim
pescar	to fish
quedarse	to stay, remain
sacar fotografías	to take photos
tomar el sol	to sunbathe
viajar	to travel

Miscellaneous:

por	for, by
a pie	on foot